Genesis Reloaded:
Uncovering the
Story of Redemption

Bible Study That Builds Christian Community

Genesis Reloaded: Uncovering the Story of Redemption
Group Member Book
© 2006 Serendipity House

Published by Serendipity House Publishers
Nashville, Tennessee

All rights reserved. No part of this work may be reproduced, stored in a retrieval
system, or transmitted in any form or by any means, electronic or mechanical,
including photocopying and recording, without express written permission of the
publisher. Requests for permission should be addressed to
Serendipity House, 117 10th Avenue North, Nashville, TN 37234.

ISBN: 1-5749-4291-3

Dewey Decimal Classification: 222.11
Subject Headings:
BIBLE. O.T. GENESIS—STUDY/ CHRISTIAN LIFE

Unless otherwise indicated, all Scripture quotations are taken from the
Holman Christian Standard Bible®. Copyright © 1999, 2000, 2002, 2003 by
Holman Bible Publishers. Used by permission.

Scriptures marked NIV are taken from the *Holy Bible*,
New International Version®, Copyright © 1973, 1978, 1984
by International Bible Society. Used by permission.

To purchase additional copies of this resource or other studies:
ORDER ONLINE at www.SerendipityHouse.com;
WRITE Serendipity House, 117 10th Avenue North, Nashville, TN 37234
FAX (615) 277-8181
PHONE (800) 525-9563

1-800-525-9563
www.SerendipityHouse.com

Printed in the United States of America
12 11 10 09 08 07 06   1 2 3 4 5 6 7 8 9 10

Contents

Core Values

Community: The purpose of this curriculum is to build community within the body of believers around Jesus Christ.

Group Process: To build community, the curriculum must be designed to take a group through a step-by-step process of sharing your story with one another.

Interactive Bible Study: To share your "story," the approach to Scripture in the curriculum needs to be open-ended and right-brained—to "level the playing field" and encourage everyone to share.

Developmental Stages: To provide a healthy program in the life cycle of a group, the curriculum needs to offer courses on three levels of commitment:

(1) **Beginner Level**—low-level entry, high structure, to level the playing field;
(2) **Growth Level**—deeper Bible study, flexible structure, to encourage group accountability;
(3) **Discipleship Level**—in-depth Bible study, open structure, to move the group into high gear.

Target Audiences: To build community throughout the culture of the church, the curriculum needs to be flexible, adaptable, and transferable into the structure of the average church.

Mission: To expand the kingdom of God one person at a time by filling the "empty chair." (We add an extra chair to each group session to remind us of our mission.)

Group Covenant

It is important that your group covenant together, agreeing to live out important group values. Once these values are agreed upon, your group will be on its way to experiencing Christian community. It's very important that your group discuss these values—preferably as you begin this study. The first session would be most appropriate. (Check the rules to which each member of your group agrees.)

- ☐ **Priority:** While you are in this course of study, you give the group meetings priority.
- ☐ **Participation:** Everyone is encouraged to participate and no one dominates.
- ☐ **Respect:** Everyone is given the right to his or her own opinion, and all questions are encouraged and respected.
- ☐ **Confidentiality:** Anything that is said in the meeting is never repeated outside the meeting.
- ☐ **Life Change:** We will regularly assess our own life-change goals and encourage one another in our pursuit of becoming more like Christ.
- ☐ **Empty Chair:** The group stays open to reaching new people at every meeting.
- ☐ **Care and Support:** Permission is given to call upon each other at any time, especially in times of crisis. The group will provide care for every member.
- ☐ **Accountability:** We agree to let the members of the group hold us accountable to the commitments we make in whatever loving ways we decide upon.
- ☐ **Mission:** We will do everything in our power to start a new group.
- ☐ **Ministry:** Members of the group will encourage one another to volunteer and serve in a ministry and to support missions by giving financially and/or personally serving.

notes

Image Is Everything

Genesis 1:26 – 2:3

Prepare for the Session

	READINGS	REFLECTIVE QUESTIONS
Monday	Genesis 1:26	Does the idea that you were made in God's image make you feel more affirmed or more challenged and responsible? In what way?
Tuesday	Genesis 1:27	How do you see God reflected in the qualities most often displayed in people of the opposite sex?
Wednesday	Genesis 1:28	What can you do to help make the world better for your children?
Thursday	Genesis 1:29-30	Are you trusting God's provision for your basic needs?
Friday	Genesis 1:31	Do you feel that the life God has given you is still good? Why or why not? What are you doing to thank God for the goodness you do find in life?
Saturday	Genesis 2:1-3	Are you taking time in your life to rest and restore your spirit? If not, what can you do to make this lifestyle change?
Sunday	Psalm 8:3-5	When you take time to reflect on creation, how does it make you feel about yourself? How does it make you feel about the God who made it all?

OUR GOALS FOR THIS SESSION ARE:

BIBLE STUDY

· To consider what being created in the image of God means
· To look at my responsibilities as a steward of the world God has created
· To better understand what I need to do to restore God's image within me

LIFE CHANGE

· To turn my life over to the lordship of Jesus Christ
· To look for someone each day to whom I can show a simple act of love
· To make a change in something I do to help take care of the environment

Icebreaker

10-15 minutes

GATHERING:
In groups of 6-8, gather people in a horseshoe configuration.

A "Chip off the Old Block." Depending on time, choose one or two questions, or answer all three. Go around the group on question 1 and let everyone share. Then go around again on question 2 and 3.

1. Who in your family do people say you most resemble physically? In what features do they see this resemblance?

2. Were someone to say, "You're just like your dad," to what feature or personal characteristic would he most likely be referring?

   ☐ My facial features
   ☐ My sense of humor
   ☐ My temper
   ☐ My way of relating to the opposite sex
   ☐ My way of saying certain things
   ☐ My way of expressing anger or dealing with conflict
   ☐ My values
   ☐ "They better not say that if they want to live!"
   ☐ Other: _____

3. What personal characteristic or physical feature of yours would you most like to see replicated in someone else in your family, such as a child or grandchild?

Bible Study
30-45 minutes

The Scripture for this week:

LEARNING FROM THE BIBLE

GENESIS 1:26 – 2:3

26Then God said, "Let Us make man in Our image, according to Our likeness. They will rule the fish of the sea, the birds of the sky, the animals, all the earth, and the creatures that crawl on the earth."

27So God created man in His own image;
He created him in the image of God;
He created them male and female.

28God blessed them, and God said to them, "Be fruitful, multiply, fill the earth, and subdue it. Rule the fish of the sea, the birds of the sky, and every creature that crawls on the earth." 29God also said, "Look, I have given you every seed-bearing plant on the surface of the entire earth, and every tree whose fruit contains seed. This food will be for you, 30for all the wildlife of the earth, for every bird of the sky, and for every creature that crawls on the earth—everything having the breath of life in it. I have given every green plant for food." And it was so. 31God saw all that He had made, and it was very good. Evening came, and then morning: the sixth day.

Chapter 2

1So the heavens and the earth and everything in them were completed. 2By the seventh day, God completed His work that He had done, and He rested on the seventh day from all His work that He had done. 3God blessed the seventh day and declared it holy, for on it He rested from His work of creation.

...about today's session

**A WORD
FROM THE
LEADER**

**Write your
answers
here.**

1. How does God understand the feeling we get when what we thought was a good file turns out to be corrupted?

2. What acts show that we are not reflecting a "clean copy" of God's image?

    a. _____

    b. _____

3. What does "Genesis" mean?

Identifying with the Story

1. What do you remember making or creating that really said something about who you are?

   ☐ A project at work
   ☐ A home remodeling project
   ☐ A poem, story, or piece of creative writing
   ☐ A craft project
   ☐ A restored automobile
   ☐ A meal or special dish
   ☐ My child
   ☐ Other: _____

2. Where in your life do you most feel like you "rule"?

   ☐ Nowhere
   ☐ When I am home alone . . . but then there's my cat.
   ☐ In my family
   ☐ When I am playing my sport
   ☐ When I am on the road in my car
   ☐ When I am at work

☐ When I am out hunting
☐ Only in my dreams
☐ Everywhere I go, I rule!
☐ Other: _____

3. When you need to rest or restore your life energy, what are you most likely to do?

☐ Read
☐ Lie on the couch and watch TV
☐ Get out into nature
☐ Go to my room and meditate or pray
☐ Lock myself in the bathroom
☐ Go for a drive
☐ Surf the internet or play computer games
☐ Go shopping
☐ Do gardening or yardwork
☐ Write in my journal
☐ Go to bed early or take a nap
☐ Other: _____

today's session

What is God teaching you from this story?

1. In general, what was humankind "born" to do?

2. What does it say to us that the last part of verse 27 refers to both males and females?

3. What are three ways we are created to reflect God's image spiritually?

a. _____

b. _____

c. _____

4. What are some destructive ways people have used their power of choice?

a. _____

b. _____

c. _____

d. _____

e. _____

5. Why is Jesus important in helping us restore the image of God within us?

Learning from the Story

1. How do you feel about God's commissioning of humankind to "rule" the plants, animals, and other life forms?

☐ What was God thinking?
☐ It's more responsibility than I want.
☐ It shows we can do whatever we want with the world.
☐ It makes me feel trusted.
☐ It makes me feel guilty—we have done such a bad job!
☐ God must believe we can do it.
☐ Other: _____

2. What do you see as the most important implication of the idea that we were made in God's image?

☐ None of us is "trash"—we all have great value.
☐ We have a lot to live up to.
☐ We can do better than we are doing.
☐ We should always look for that image of God in ourselves and in others.
☐ We will be happiest if we live as we were created to live.
☐ Other: _____

3. In what way have you recently seen the image of God reflected in yourself or in someone close to you?

life change lessons

How can you apply this session to your life?

1. Since no one has ever seen God, what does John tell us that we need to do?

Write your answers here.

2. According to John, how do the people we are now compare with the people we will be one day?

Caring Time
15-20 minutes

CARING TIME

This is the time to develop and express your care for each other. Begin by asking group members to respond to this question:

◯ Remain in groups of 6-8 people, in a horseshoe configuration.

"How can this group show love to you right now?"

Pray for love and direction in these areas of need, as well as for the concerns on the Prayer/Praise Report. Include prayer for the empty chair.

If you would like to pray silently, say "Amen" when you have finished your prayer, so that the next person will know when to start.

Reference Notes

Use these notes to gain further understanding
of the text as you study on your own:

GENESIS
1:26

image ... likeness. God created people to be like Him. Adam and Eve
became unlike God only when they tried to be "like" Him in terms
of authority (see Gen. 3:5). Romans 8:29 reminds us that it is still
God's intention to make us into His likeness, that likeness revealed in
Jesus Christ.

GENESIS
1:27

male and female. Who of us is not aware of the differences between men
and women? And yet, both were created in the image of God and given
the responsibility to take care of the earth. In how men and women relate
to each other, we are different; in how we relate to God, we are the same
(see Gal. 3:28).

GENESIS
1:28

rule. God gave people the responsibility to rule over the world. Ruling
over and subduing is not an invitation to exploit. It does not make us sov-
ereign over all; rather, we are stewards, ruling on God's behalf (see Christ's
Parable of the Tenants, Matt. 21:33-42).

GENESIS
1:31

very good ... sixth day. This last day of creation was not just described
as "good," but "very good." It was the culmination of God's work in creating our world. It was an apt description of the world God intended for us
to live in and wanted us to have.

GENESIS
2:3

He rested. Even though we see God's energy as unlimited, Scripture
proclaims that even God took time to rest from His creative work. When
God gave the Ten Commandments, He referred back to this: "Remember
to dedicate the Sabbath day" (Ex. 20:8).

notes

notes

Session

2

Expecting Company

Genesis 2:18-25

Prepare for the Session

	READINGS	REFLECTIVE QUESTIONS
Monday	Genesis 2:18	How do you handle being alone?
Tuesday	Genesis 2:19-20	What does it mean to you that God included Adam in the process of naming the animals?
Wednesday	Genesis 2:21-23	In what ways are persons of the opposite sex like you, and in what ways are they different? What can you learn from them?
Thursday	Genesis 2:24	How difficult has it been to separate yourself from your father and mother? Why?
Friday	Genesis 2:25	How do you feel about your body and your role as a sexual being? What would help you feel more at ease with yourself in this area of your life?
Saturday	1 Corinthians 11:11-12	How do you react in situations where you have to depend on the opposite sex? Why do we need to learn to depend on one another?
Sunday	Ephesians 5:28-32	How has God used your relationship with your spouse or another member of the opposite sex to teach you about His relationship with you?

BIBLE STUDY

- To explore what Genesis means when it says that it is not good for people to be alone
- To better understand the community God created for humankind and desires for us today
- To consider ways you might help restore community to our world

LIFE CHANGE

- To help someone you have not helped before
- To reveal one aspect about yourself in this or another trusted group
- To set aside time to spend with a lonely person

Icebreaker
10-15 minutes

GATHERING:
In groups of 6-8, gather people in a horseshoe configuration.

Love Me, Love My Dog. Depending on time, choose one or two questions, or answer all three. Go around the group on question 1 and let everyone share. Then go around again on question 2 and 3.

1. When you look back at the pets (or farm animals) you had as a child, which would you say was your favorite? Why?

2. As a child, if you could have had any animal you wanted as a pet, what animal would you have chosen?

   ☐ A cat   ☐ A dolphin (in our swimming pool!)
   ☐ A dog   ☐ A tiger
   ☐ A horse   ☐ An anaconda
   ☐ A monkey   ☐ Other: _____

3. What role would you say animals play in your household now?

   ☐ Our pets are part of the family.
   ☐ "The more people I meet, the more I love my dog!"
   ☐ We are into stuffed animals—they're easier to care for.

18

☐ We love animals so much we're vegetarian.

☐ Our animals have trained us well.

☐ We have no animals in our family—well, except for a few of my in-laws!

☐ Other: _____

Bible Study

30-45 minutes

The Scripture for this week:

LEARNING FROM THE BIBLE

GENESIS 2:18-25

[18]Then the LORD God said, "It is not good for the man to be alone. I will make a helper who is like him." [19]So the LORD God formed out of the ground each wild animal and each bird of the sky, and brought each to the man to see what he would call it. And whatever the man called a living creature, that was its name. [20]The man gave names to all the livestock, to the birds of the sky, and to every wild animal; but for the man no helper was found who was like him. [21]So the LORD God caused a deep sleep to come over the man, and he slept. God took one of his ribs and closed the flesh at that place. [22]Then the LORD God made the rib He had taken from the man into a woman and brought her to the man [23]And the man said:

This one, at last, is bone of my bone, and flesh of my flesh; this one will be called woman, for she was taken from man.

[24]This is why a man leaves his father and mother and bonds with his wife, and they become one flesh. [25]Both the man and his wife were naked, yet felt no shame.

...about today's session

A WORD FROM THE LEADER

Write your answers here.

1. What are some of the actions people take to disrupt the community God wants us to have?

   a. _____

   b. _____

   c. _____

   d. _____

   e. _____

2. What good news do you see today in relation to our desire for human community?

a. _____

b. _____

c. _____

3. How was the oneness which Genesis speaks about as existing between the man and the woman damaged by the time Christ came? How did Christ redeem this area of life?

Identifying with the Story

1. Which of the following activities do you remember doing with "the dust of the ground" when you were a child in grade school?

☐ Making mud pies
☐ Helping with a garden
☐ Burying a treasure
☐ Chasing ants
☐ Ruining my "school" clothes
☐ Avoiding it—even then I was a clean freak!
☐ Other _____

2. If you could have a friend "custom designed" to fit your social needs, what would that person be like?

3. What would you say was the loneliest time of your life? What made that time so lonely?

What is God teaching you from this story?

1. What makes it evident that Adam needed help with something other than just physical labor?

2. What was unique about Eve that made her especially suited for community with Adam?

2

3. Give an Old Testament example of two people who felt a spiritual oneness with each other.

4. In the New Testament, how was spiritual oneness shown by the way people talked about each other?

5. What are two aspects of what we might call "relational nakedness"?

    a. _____

    b. _____

Learning from the Story

♘ Remain in groups of 6-8 people, in a horseshoe configuration.

1. Why do you think God gave Adam the privilege of naming the animals?

  ☐ The children always get to name the pets!
  ☐ It was a way of including him in the creative process.
  ☐ It showed he really was in charge.
  ☐ If he named the animals, he would be more likely to be a good steward over them.
  ☐ Other: _____

2. How did the method God used to create the woman differ from how He created the animals? Why is this difference important?

3. If you could ask God to do something to help you with your own loneliness, as He helped Adam with his, what would it be?

life change lessons

**How can you
apply this
session to
your life?**

**Write your
answers
here.**

1. Give two misperceptions about community we may be tempted to believe?

    a. _____

    b. _____

2. What does the kingdom of God in its fullness bring that will lead to perfect community?

    a. _____

    b. _____

Caring Time
15-20 minutes

**CARING
TIME**

⟲**Remain
in groups of
6-8 people, in
a horseshoe
configuration.**

This is the time to develop and express your care for each other. Begin by asking group members to respond to this question:

"How can this group serve as a helper to you right now?"

Pray for the needs mentioned, as well as the concerns on the Prayer/Praise Report. Include prayer for the empty chair.

If you would like to pray silently, say "Amen" when you have finished your prayer, so that the next person will know when to start.

Reference Notes

Use these notes to gain further understanding
of the text as you study on your own:

**GENESIS
2:18**

not good for the man to be alone. God made people to need each other.
One of the reasons for this is the practical matter of procreation. God is a
creative God. He created the plants with seeds to procreate. He created a
man and then a woman to bring children into the world. But He also created her to bring a more in-depth companionship than Adam could have
with the animals.

**GENESIS
2:19**

out of the ground. This also was how Adam himself had been formed
(see Gen. 2:7).

**GENESIS
2:20**

the man gave names to all the livestock. This was Adam's first act of
stewardship over the earth—naming the animals. First, God had named
the elements: the sun, the moon, the sky, and the land. Then God allowed
Adam to name the living creatures.

no helper was found who was like him. Animals can help humankind
in many different ways. Horses and donkeys can carry our loads; birds
can bring peace with their songs; dogs can be taught to retrieve the morning paper. But none of these are *like* us; with none of them can we find the
commonality necessary for true community.

**GENESIS
2:24**

leaves ... bonds. From the beginning of creation, God established the
order of the family. Just as Eve was made from Adam's own body, so when
a couple is married, the two become one. A man leaves his home (as a
woman also leaves hers), the roots from which he or she came, and estab-
lishes a new life with a new family. Even though polygamy is practiced
in the Old Testament, it is clear from this verse that God's plan was for a
man and a woman to become one in a lifelong service and union that is
monogamous.

**GENESIS
2:25**

no shame. It is difficult to imagine a world with no shame, a completely
innocent world. Yet this is the world that God provided for Adam and Eve.
This gives a wonderful picture of God's plan for people: a plan that was
soon to be ruined by the arrival of sin.

notes

3

Tripped Up

Genesis 3:1-24

Prepare for the Session

	READINGS	REFLECTIVE QUESTIONS
Monday	Genesis 3:1-5	What rationalizations do you use when you want to do something God has said is wrong?
Tuesday	Genesis 3:6	Think about a time when you were deceived by appearances. What elements in your character made you vulnerable to this sort of deception?
Wednesday	Genesis 3:7	When have your eyes been opened to something about yourself that embarrassed you? Did you act to correct what embarrassed you?
Thursday	Genesis 3:8	In what ways have you tried to hide from God? What actions or aspects of your personality would you rather God not discover?
Friday	Genesis 3:9-13	Is there shame in your life? What is the source of shame?
Saturday	Genesis 3:14-19	How are you paying now for past mistakes? How have you put past mistakes to good use?
Sunday	Genesis 3:20-24	How have you felt left out of the plan? How has God taken measures to include you in the redemptive story?

BIBLE STUDY

- To understand how humankind lost the paradise God created for us
- To consider the punishments which came because of sin
- To look at what it means to repent and find God's grace

LIFE CHANGE

- To choose a trusted Christian friend to serve as a confidant
- To identify persons who have been tempters in your life and avoid them
- To spend time in prayer at the end of each day

Icebreaker
10-15 minutes

**GATHERING:
In groups
of 6-8, gather
people in a
horseshoe
configuration.**

Busted! Depending on time, choose one or two questions, or answer all three. Go around the group on question 1 and let everyone share. Then go around again on question 2 and 3.

1. What is your most vivid memory of being discovered by a parent or guardian while involved in some kind of wrong behavior?

2. When you got into trouble as a child or adolescent, whom did you most frequently blame?

   ☐ A sibling
   ☐ A friend
   ☐ A rival
   ☐ Circumstances
   ☐ The devil
   ☐ A pet
   ☐ Myself
   ☐ Other: _____

3. What could you most easily get "busted" for as an adult?

☐ Snacking between meals or breaking my diet
☐ Leaving work early
☐ Playing computer games at work
☐ Speeding
☐ Flirting
☐ Illegally downloading songs or movies
☐ Dozing during the sermon
☐ Talking on my cell phone while driving
☐ Other: _____

Bible Study

30-45 minutes

The Scripture for this week:

LEARNING FROM THE BIBLE

GENESIS 3:1-24

¹Now the serpent was the most cunning of all the wild animals that the LORD God had made. He said to the woman, "Did God really say, 'You can't eat from any tree in the garden'?" ²The woman said to the serpent, "We may eat the fruit from the trees in the garden. ³But about the fruit of the tree in the middle of the garden, God said, 'You must not eat it or touch it, or you will die.' " ⁴"No! You will not die," the serpent said to the woman. ⁵"In fact, God knows that when you eat it your eyes will be opened and you will be like God, knowing good and evil." ⁶Then the woman saw that the tree was good for food and delightful to look at, and that it was desirable for obtaining wisdom. So she took some of its fruit and ate it; she also gave some to her husband, who was with her, and he ate it. ⁷Then the eyes of both of them were opened, and they knew they were naked; so they sewed fig leaves together and made loincloths for themselves.

Sin's Consequences

⁸Then the man and his wife heard the sound of the LORD God walking in the garden at the time of the evening breeze, and they hid themselves from the LORD God among the trees of the garden. ⁹So the LORD God called out to the man and said to him, "Where are you?" ¹⁰And he said, "I heard You in the garden, and I was afraid because

27

I was naked, so I hid." ¹¹Then He asked, "Who told you that you were naked? Did you eat from the tree that I had commanded you not to eat from?" ¹²Then the man replied, "The woman You gave to be with me—she gave me some fruit from the tree, and I ate." ¹³So the LORD God asked the woman, "What is this you have done?" And the woman said, "It was the serpent. He deceived me, and I ate." ¹⁴Then the LORD God said to the serpent: Because you have done this, you are cursed more than any livestock and more than any wild animal. You will move on your belly and eat dust all the days of your life. ¹⁵I will put hostility between you and the woman, and between your seed and her seed. He will strike your head, and you will strike his heel. ¹⁶He said to the woman: I will intensify your labor pains; you will bear children in anguish. Your desire will be for your husband, yet he will dominate you. ¹⁷And He said to Adam, "Because you listened to your wife's voice and ate from the tree about which I commanded you, 'Do not eat from it': The ground is cursed because of you. You will eat from it by means of painful labor all the days of your life. ¹⁸It will produce thorns and thistles for you, and you will eat the plants of the field. ¹⁹You will eat bread by the sweat of your brow until you return to the ground, since you were taken from it. For you are dust, and you will return to dust." ²⁰Adam named his wife Eve because she was the mother of all the living. ²¹The LORD God made clothing out of skins for Adam and his wife, and He clothed them. ²²The LORD God said, "Since man has become like one of Us, knowing good and evil, he must not reach out, and also take from the tree of life, and eat, and live forever." ²³So the LORD God sent him away from the Garden of Eden to work the ground from which he was taken. ²⁴He drove man out, and east of the Garden of Eden He stationed cherubim with a flaming, whirling sword to guard the way to the tree of life.

...about today's session

**A WORD
FROM THE
LEADER**

**Write your
answers
here.**

1. What are three things we often mourn which were part of the paradise Adam and Eve lost?

   a. _____

   b. _____

   c. _____

2. What are three attitudes we can have toward the fact that we have lost this paradise?

    a. _____

    b. _____

    c. _____

3. What problems can come from looking at the present world with rose-colored glasses?

Identifying with the Story

⋃ **Remain in groups of ⅝-8 people, in a horseshoe configuration.**

1. Describe a time when you found yourself in hot water as a result of accepting bad advice.

2. What kind of labor are you looking at as especially "punishing" right now?

    ☐ The labor of birth (I'm expecting!)
    ☐ All the paperwork I have to go through at work
    ☐ All the paperwork I have to go through at home
    ☐ Yard work that needs to be done
    ☐ The drudgery of regular housework
    ☐ Special projects around the house
    ☐ Mental work – figuring out how to approach problems
    ☐ Emotional/ relational work – dealing with people
    ☐ Physical labor that my body is no longer up to
    ☐ Other: _____

3. Where do you most see yourself in this story right now?

☐ Feeling the lure of temptation in my life (vv. 1-6)
☐ Feeling that my eyes have recently been opened to what the world really is (v. 7)
☐ Feeling like my eyes have recently been opened to my own nakedness and shame (v. 7)
☐ Finding myself hiding from God (v. 8)
☐ Feeling overwhelmed by blame and responsibility (vv. 11-13)
☐ Feeling like I'm "eating other people's dust" (v. 14)
☐ Finding myself caught up in hostility (v. 15)
☐ Feeling dominated in my relationships (v. 16)
☐ Feeling like an exile from home (v. 24)
☐ Other: _____

today's session

**What is God
teaching you
from this
story?**

1. The world Adam and Eve found themselves in after their sin was far different from the Garden of Eden. Name three ways it was different.

a. _____

b. _____

c. _____

2. What were three results of human sin in the lives of Adam and Eve?

a. _____

b. _____

c. _____

3. How did Adam and Eve's sin affect their attitude toward their own nakedness?

4. Besides Adam and Eve, what other Old Testament character tried to hide from God, but found he could not?

5. What is one good answer to the question, "Why does life have to be so hard?"

Learning from the Story

⊖ Remain in groups of -8 people, in a horseshoe configuration.

1. Why was the serpent so effective in its bid to tempt Eve?

2. What seems to be Adam and Eve's main motivation for hiding among the trees of the Garden?

☐ Modesty—they didn't want to be seen naked
☐ Fear—they were trying to avoid punishment
☐ Shame—they didn't want to face up to what they had done
☐ Other: _____

3. What is your own most common reaction when you know you've done something wrong?

☐ I rationalize why I have done it (vv. 4-5).
☐ I try to avoid God (v. 8).
☐ I find someone to blame (vv. 12-13).
☐ Me, do something wrong?!
☐ I own up to my guilt.
☐ I go immediately to God in prayer and ask forgiveness.
☐ Other: _____

life change lessons

How can you apply this session to your life?

Write your answers here.

1. What three actions need to be part of true life change?

   a. _____

   b. _____

   c. _____

2. What must repentance include besides just saying you are sorry?

Caring Time

15-20 minutes

CARING TIME

♘ Remain in groups of 6-8 people, in a horseshoe configuration.

This is the time to develop and express your care for each other. Begin by asking group members to respond to this question:

"Where in your life are you being tempted and needing strength?"

Pray for strength and direction in these areas, as well as for the concerns on the Prayer/Praise Report. Include prayer for the empty chair.

If you would like to pray silently, say "Amen" when you have finished your prayer, so that the next person will know when to start.

Reference Notes

BIBLE STUDY NOTES

Use these notes to gain further understanding of the text as you study on your own:

GENESIS 3:1-3

"Did God really say, 'You can't eat ...'" The serpent took a partial truth and twisted it around. God did not say they weren't to eat from any tree in the garden (2:16). But He told them not to eat from the one tree, the tree of the knowledge of good and evil (2:17). Eve had understood the prohibition correctly.

GENESIS 3:4   *"You will not die."* Jesus said that lies are Satan's native tongue (John 8:44). In Eve's case, the serpent's lie was in saying that God did not really mean what He said. Satan still uses that device today, trying to get people to distrust God's Word.

GENESIS 3:5   *"You will be like God."* The ultimate sin of humankind is trying to be like God. It was also the sin that was made manifest at the Tower of Babel (Gen. 11:1-9).

GENESIS 3:6   *good ... delightful ... desirable.* Temptation has not changed over thousands of years. The New Testament describes the basic components as "the lust of the flesh, the lust of the eyes, and the pride in one's lifestyle" (1 John 2:16). Basically, the serpent told Eve that the fruit would taste good ("the lust of the flesh"), that it looked good ("the lust of the eyes"), and that it would make her wiser (giving her pride).

GENESIS 3:7   *made loincloths for themselves.* Adam and Eve had not gained great wisdom from the fruit; they had only succeeded in disobeying God and realizing the shame and guilt of that disobedience. With the advent of sin, everything looked different. Previously they had felt no shame at their nakedness (Gen. 2:25); but sin had now polluted their perception and made them feel bad about their bodies. But covering themselves could not hide their disobedience and remove their guilt.

GENESIS 3:8   *they hid.* Adam and Eve foolishly tried to hide from the God who knew everything about them. The One who was the source of everything they needed was the One from whom they were hiding. Sin had disrupted their relationship with God. People still think they can hide from God, but their efforts to do so are just as futile.

GENESIS 3:9   *"Where are you?"* God's goal is always to connect with us. He could have gone to where Adam and Eve were hiding, for He obviously knew where they were. However, He invited them to respond to Him. God immediately began to seek those who were lost.

GENESIS 3:12   *"The woman You gave to be with me ..."* Adam did what is natural for most people. He not only passed the blame, but ultimately blamed God for his own disobedience. Adam refused to take responsibility for his own actions.

GENESIS 3:13   *"He deceived me."* Eve, when given the blame by Adam, then passed it on to the serpent. While it was true that the serpent had told her a lie, she was at fault for being willing to take the serpent's word over God's. She made a wrong choice and needed to own up to it.

GENESIS 3:15   *strike your head ... strike his heal.* This is sometimes considered the first prophecy of Christ's work. In Adam's sin and in Christ's death, Satan dealt a blow (he would "strike his heal," a harmful, but ultimately not deadly wound). However, in the resurrection, Christ struck Satan's "head," for He completely destroyed the work of Satan.

labor pains ... Your desire will be for your husband. Eve did not lose all the good in life when she lost her innocence. She still would bear children and love her husband. But with the knowledge of good and evil came a price. Children would bring pain as well as joy. Sexual relations would be a power over her, not just love and intimacy.

by means of painful labor. Again, there would be a price to be paid for the good in life. Adam was still able to grow food and feed himself and his family. But now that task meant painful and difficult labor. His dominion over the earth would be a struggle that would end in death.

dust. Adam's life and sustenance came from the ground. In his death he would return to the same state.

made clothing out of skins. God meets us in our disobedience. He does not merely stand back and say, "So, what are you going to do now?" He covered Adam and Eve. In His grace, God meets humankind in our sinful state and provides what we need.

good and evil. Before eating from the forbidden tree, Adam and Eve knew good. They knew God. How amazing it would be to live in a world where good was the only reality. After the fall into sin, however, Adam and Eve discovered evil and its deadly consequences (Rom. 5:12; 6:23).

sent him away. This was the deciding moment. The man and woman were ejected from the garden, from the tree of life, and from delightful, comfortable walks with God. They were not robbed of life immediately, but were banished to an eventual death. God had to send them from the garden because they could not, in their sinful state, eat from the tree of life and live forever.

cherubim. Cherubim are winged angels. In Ezekiel 10, Ezekiel described his vision that included cherubim.

tree of life. Sin destroyed people's access to the tree of life and the eternal life for which God created us, but that access will be restored in the new heaven and earth (Rev. 2:7; 22:1-2,14,19).

notes

notes

4

Enter Conflict

Genesis 4:1-16

Prepare for the Session

	READINGS	REFLECTIVE QUESTIONS
Monday	Genesis 4:1-2	How do you help others—particularly your family—in the important discovery of their gifts and abilities?
Tuesday	Genesis 4:3-5	When was the last time you were angry towards God for something you thought was unfair? How well do you know God's heart?
Wednesday	Genesis 4:6-7	In what ways has your anger led you to betray your heart? How can you handle your anger in a way that will produce more positive results?
Thursday	Genesis 4:8	In what ways have you "attacked" a Christian brother or sister recently? Why did you do so? What damage did your attack cause? How can you make amends?
Friday	Genesis 4:9	In what ways do you need to behave more responsibly toward those close to you? How much responsibility do you have for others?
Saturday	Genesis 4:10-12	How have you suffered as a result of the way you have treated someone? Was the suffering deserved? Why or why not?
Sunday	Genesis 4:13-16	Have you ever felt like God protected you from the consequences of your mistakes? In what way?

BIBLE STUDY

· To learn how violence entered the world through Cain's murder of Abel
· To better understand how violence spreads, and what we can do to stop the spread
· To see how verbal violence can also be destructive, and to find healthy ways of expressing anger

LIFE CHANGE

· To ask forgiveness for any violent words we have spoken
· To explore non-destructive ways to express our anger
· To affirm someone we consider to be a rival for an achievement

Icebreaker
10-15 minutes

**GATHERING:
In groups
of 6-8, gather
people in a
horseshoe
configuration.**

Sibling Rivalry. Depending on time, choose one or two questions, or answer all three. Go around the group on question 1 and let everyone share. Then go around again on question 2 and 3.

1. As a child or adolescent, what do you remember fighting over with someone who was either a sibling or like a sibling to you?

   ☐ Parental attention   ☐ Favorite food
   ☐ A particular game or toy   ☐ Family pet
   ☐ Almost everything   ☐ Almost nothing
   ☐ Other: _____

2. Who is your biggest rival as an adult?

   ☐ Still my sibling
   ☐ My spouse
   ☐ Someone at work
   ☐ My spouse's ex
   ☐ A really competitive friend
   ☐ There are no rivals
   ☐ Other: _____

3. When you get in a situation in which you feel you are competing with a rival, how do you tend to react?

☐ Go for the jugular!
☐ Well, I'm competitive, but not all that vicious...most of the time.
☐ I like to win, but it's all in good fun.
☐ I look for "win-win."
☐ I try not to make it a contest at all.
☐ I give in rather than compete.
☐ Other: _____

Bible Study
30-45 minutes 4

The Scripture for this week:

LEARNING FROM THE BIBLE

GENESIS 4:1-16

¹Adam knew his wife Eve intimately, and she conceived and gave birth to Cain. She said, "I have had a male child with the LORD's help." ²Then she also gave birth to his brother Abel. Now Abel became a shepherd of a flock, but Cain cultivated the land. ³In the course of time Cain presented some of the land's produce as an offering to the LORD. ⁴And Abel also presented [an offering] —some of the firstborn of his flock and their fat portions. The LORD had regard for Abel and his offering, ⁵but He did not have regard for Cain and his offering. Cain was furious, and he was downcast. ⁶Then the LORD said to Cain, "Why are you furious? And why are you downcast? ⁷If you do right, won't you be accepted? But if you do not do right, sin is crouching at the door. Its desire is for you, but you must master it." ⁸Cain said to his brother Abel, "Let's go out to the field." And while they were in the field, Cain attacked his brother Abel and killed him. ⁹Then the LORD said to Cain, "Where is your brother Abel?" "I don't know," he replied. "Am I my brother's guardian?" ¹⁰Then He said, "What have you done? Your brother's blood cries out to Me from the ground! ¹¹So now you are cursed [with alienation] from the ground that opened its mouth to receive your brother's blood you have shed. ¹²If you work the land, it will never again give you its yield. You will be a restless wanderer on the earth." ¹³But Cain answered the LORD,

"My punishment is too great to bear! [14]Since You are banishing me today from the soil, and I must hide myself from Your presence and become a restless wanderer on the earth, whoever finds me will kill me." [15]Then the LORD replied to him, "In that case, whoever kills Cain will suffer vengeance seven times over." And He placed a mark on Cain so that whoever found him would not kill him. [16]Then Cain went out from the LORD's presence and lived in the land of Nod, east of Eden.

...about today's session

A WORD
FROM THE
LEADER

Write your
answers
here.

1. What are some examples of violence found in Scripture?

   a. _____

   b. _____

   c. _____

   d. _____

   e. _____

2. How is the motivation for including violence in Scripture different from the motivation of many movie and electronic game producers for including violence?

3. How is the cure that the Bible prescribes for the violence in the world different from what some secular perspectives suggest?

Identifying with the Story

1. Think about the last time you acted to help someone only to be rejected or slighted. How did you feel? What did you do?

2. Had you been Cain in this story, how would you have reacted to God?

☐ Pouted a lot
☐ Acted like I didn't care
☐ Tried harder the next time
☐ Found out what I did wrong
☐ Decided that next time I'd give a gift certificate!
☐ Just quit trying
☐ Other: _____

3. Had you been Cain, how would you have felt about the punishment meted out against you?

☐ Grateful I got off so easy
☐ Depressed at losing my chosen profession
☐ Like nobody understood me
☐ Still a little anxious about someone killing me
☐ Reassured by God's protection
☐ Other: _____

4

today's session

What is God teaching you from this story?

1. List three contributors to the spread of violence that can be observed in this story.

   a. _____

   b. _____

   c. _____

2. What two examples of the injury-revenge cycle from the Old Testament are provided through this event?

   a. _____

   b. _____

3. About what kind of non-physical violence did Jesus worn?

4. What tendency was God counteracting when He told Cain that if he did right he would be accepted?

5. What condition does Isaiah describe as an essential part of his vision of worldwide non-violence?

Learning from the Story

1. What does the phrase, "If you do not do right, sin is crouching at the door" mean to you? How is temptation increased when a person is in a self-pitying mood?

2. How does Cain's punishment compare to that of his father Adam's (3:17-24)? What part of his punishment do you think was most difficult to bear?

3. When have you been involved in a relationship where the use of cutting words (verbal violence) escalated? Have you found a way to escape the cycle yet? If so, how did you do it?

life change lessons

How can you
apply this
session to
your life?

Write your
answers
here.

1. What are two lessons we should learn from Cain's mistake?

   a. _____

   b. _____

2. According to Paul, how can we keep anger from getting out
   of hand?

   a. _____

   b. _____

4

Caring Time

15-20 minutes

CARING
TIME

⚘ Remain
in groups of
6-8 people, in
a horseshoe
configuration.

This is the time to develop and express your care for each other.
Begin by asking group members to respond to this question:

"How are you struggling with forgivness right now?"

Pray for God's strength to forgive in these situations, as well
as praying for the concerns on the Prayer/Praise Report. Include
prayer for the empty chair.

If you would like to pray silently, say "Amen" when you have finished your prayer, so that the next person will know when to start.

Reference Notes

Use these notes to gain further understanding
of the text as you study on your own:

shepherd ... cultivated the land. Thus is set up what would become a
classic historical conflict between agriculture and those who raise livestock. This conflict was also prominent in the old American West.

firstborn ... fat portions. The conflict between the offerings of Cain and Abel was not a conflict regarding vegetables or animals. It was a matter of the attitude of the giver, one who simply brings God something (the text does not say that Cain brought the best or first fruits of his crop), versus the giver who brings God the best. Offerings to God were to be the first fruits, the best. That is why Abel brought the fat portions of the firstborn of his flock. The best always belongs to the Lord. When we give God the best, we are making a statement that we trust Him enough to offer a gift to Him first, knowing that He will care for our needs. The writer of Hebrews said that Abel's example still speaks about the kind of commitment God desires (Heb. 11:4).

**GENESIS
4:5**

Cain was furious. We learn a lot about Cain's character from his reaction to God's disapproval. Rather than seeking to learn about what God expects or learn from the example of his brother Abel, he simply got mad and pouted.

**GENESIS
4:7**

crouching. What a visual image of sin: crouching like a predatory animal, just waiting to overtake us. God knew Cain's heart, and knew that he was dangerously close to being overtaken by sin.

**GENESIS
4:8**

Cain attacked ... and killed. With malicious intent, Cain set about to rid himself of someone more favored than he. This is a sad picture of fallen humanity. Cain's concern was not to better himself in order to please God, but to bring down the competition that made him look bad. What a long way humanity had fallen in the time between Genesis 1 and Genesis 4.

**GENESIS
4:9**

"Am I my brother's guardian?" Cain sought to control this encounter by the way he set up the question. A guardian is one placed over a minor who cannot care for himself. Certainly this was not the situation with Abel. Another word often used in translations of this question is "keeper." A keeper is one who was to care for dumb or vulnerable animals. This was also not true of Abel. In fact, it was Abel who was a "keeper" of animals. But Cain was raising the wrong question, and he knew it. What he was being called to do was to be his brother's *brother*. He was called to treat his brother with love as kin. This he had obviously not done. He first lied to God, saying he did not know where Abel was. Then he sought to throw God off with an inappropriate question that only showed his lack of concern. He had no pricks of conscience regarding his brother's death.

**GENESIS
4:10**

"Your brother's blood cries out to Me." The first murder. The first human blood shed. The horror of this first murder, the taking of someone's life without remorse, reveals the depths of evil to which people can sink. Cain may have thought that he had gotten away with it, but God knew exactly what had happened—and why.

**GENESIS
4:12**

the land ... will never again give you its yield. Cain's punishment was severe. He had farmed the land, but now the land would not produce

GENESIS 4:12 (cont'd) for him. In a sense, the land which had absorbed Abel's blood that cried out to God was joining in punishing Cain because it had been forced to receive his crime.

restless wanderer. It would be one thing to choose intentionally the life of a nomad, to love the open road. But Cain had originally chosen agriculture, a profession which, as opposed to hunting, appealed to those who wanted to stay in one place. Cain would be a restless wanderer—always moving on because he did not belong, never able to go home again.

GENESIS 4:13 *too great to bear.* Cain did not cry for his brother or repent before God. His reaction showed that he thought life was still all about him.

GENESIS 4:14 *whoever finds me will kill me.* We do not know who these people are whom Cain feared, or where they may have come from. However, it is clear that Cain understood what a vicious cycle of violence he had let loose. Violence would beget violence.

GENESIS 4:15 *whoever kills Cain ...* God was not so much seeking to protect Cain as seeking to short circuit a cycle of violence.

He placed a mark on Cain. We do not know what this mark was, but it was an identifiable sign that he was under divine protection.

4

notes

5

A Watery Judgment

Genesis 6:11-22

Prepare for the Session

	READINGS	REFLECTIVE QUESTIONS
Monday	Genesis 6:11-13	How does bad news affect your family? How has it changed how you live your life?
Tuesday	Genesis 6:14-16	How clear are you concerning what God is calling you to do at this point in your life? If He gave you an exact blueprint, would it reassure or intimidate you?
Wednesday	Genesis 6:17-18	What does it mean that God has established His covenant with you? Why is it important that God initiated this covenant?
Thursday	Genesis 6:19-21	How are you doing at caring for the life that has been put under your care? What do you do when your responsibilities just seem to be too much to handle?
Friday	Genesis 6:22	Is it hard or easy for you to obey God? In what way does your pride get in the way of obedience?
Saturday	Hebrews 11:7	Would you have enough faith to follow God anywhere if you were certain God was calling you?
Sunday	2 Peter 2:4-9	Do you take seriously God's power and right to judge sin? How does that affect the way you live daily?

BIBLE STUDY
- To consider why God sent the great flood
- To better understand why God judges human behavior
- To appreciate the grace God always shows in the midst of judgment

LIFE CHANGE
- To model non-violent solutions to conflict in our home
- To have our own weekly "judgment day"
- To be an "ark" to rescue someone else

Icebreaker

10-15 minutes

GATHERING:
In groups of 6-8, gather people in a horseshoe configuration.

Under Construction. Depending on time, choose one or two questions, or answer all three. Go around the group on question 1 and let everyone share. Then go around again on question 2 and 3.

1. What do you remember having the most fun making or building when you were in grade school?

   ☐ A tree house
   ☐ A fort out of sheets and blankets in my room
   ☐ A birdhouse
   ☐ Projects with plastic building blocks
   ☐ A soapbox derby car
   ☐ Cakes for a party
   ☐ My collection of stuffed animals
   ☐ A snowman or snow fort
   ☐ A "secret" hideout
   ☐ Other: _____

2. What do you have that is "under construction" in your life right now?

   ☐ A home addition or improvement   ☐ My career
   ☐ My Christian walk   ☐ A new self-image
   ☐ My marriage   ☐ A car I'm rebuilding
   ☐ A relationship   ☐ A business
   ☐ Other: _____

3. What would you say is your most essential "building tool" right now?

☐ The patience I have for the building process
☐ My self-confidence
☐ The reservoir of friends I have to help
☐ The skills God has given me
☐ My creativity
☐ My willingness to follow a plan or blueprint
☐ My perfectionistic desire to get things right
☐ Other: _____

Bible Study

30-45 minutes

The Scripture for this week:

LEARNING FROM THE BIBLE

GENESIS 6:11-22

[11]Now the earth was corrupt in God's sight, and the earth w **5** *filled with violence. [12]God saw how corrupt the earth was, for all flesh had corrupted its way on the earth. [13]Then God said to Noah, "I have decided to put an end to all flesh, for the earth is filled with violence because of them; therefore I am going to destroy them along with the earth. [14]Make yourself an ark of goferwood. Make rooms in the ark, and cover it with pitch inside and outside. [15]This is how you are to make it: The ark will be 450 feet long, 75 feet wide, and 45 feet high. [16]You are to make a roof, finishing the sides of the ark] to within 18 inches of the roof. You are to put a door in the side of the ark. Make it with lower, middle, and upper [decks]. [17]Understand that I am bringing a deluge—floodwaters on the earth to destroy all flesh under heaven with the breath of life in it. Everything on earth will die. [18]But I will establish My covenant with you, and you will enter the ark with your sons, your wife, and your sons' wives. [19]You are also to bring into the ark two of every living thing of all flesh, male and female, to keep them alive with you. [20]Two of everything—from the birds according to their kinds, from the livestock according to their kinds, and from every animal that crawls on the ground according to its kind—will come to you so that you can keep them alive. [21]Take with you every kind of food that is eaten; gather it as food for you and for them." [22]And Noah did this. He did everything that God had commanded him.*

...about today's session

A WORD
FROM THE
LEADER

Write your
answers
here.

1. What are some of the different emotions God shows in the Bible?

   a. _____

   b. _____

   c. _____

   d. _____

2. What was God's emotional reaction to the corruption He saw in His creation?

3. What are two examples of flood stories in other cultures?

   a. _____

   b. _____

Identifying with the Story

**⊍ Remain
in groups of
6-8 people, in
a horseshoe
configuration.**

1. What was the worst natural disaster that you have ever been in or near? What sticks in your mind concerning this event?

2. How would you advise someone to prepare for a disaster like the one you went through? Where should he go; what should he take with him?

3. How did you understand God's role in the disaster you went through?

- ☐ God used it to show His power.
- ☐ It made me question God's goodness.
- ☐ God was there for the victims after the event.
- ☐ Nature just did what nature does—God wasn't specifically directing it.
- ☐ I really felt it was a judgment by God.
- ☐ It's just what happens in a fallen world.
- ☐ Other: _____

today's session

What is God teaching you from this story?

1. What are two ways we can misunderstand or be misled by the story of the flood?

   a. _____

   b. _____

2. What were two aspects of life on earth that God was judging through the flood?

   a. _____

   b. _____

3. Name another incident of human violence that is reported shortly after the story of Cain and Abel.

4. What is the importance of the flood story?

5. What is another biblical example of God preserving a remnant from a disaster?

Learning from the Story

U Remain in groups of 6-8 people, in a horseshoe configuration.

1. What seems to be the root of God's anger and judgment? Do you see that anger as justified?

2. Why was it important that God gave such specific instructions to Noah on how to build the ark?

3. What is the most difficult task God has called you to do? How did you do (or how are you doing) at responding to that call?

life change lessons

How can you apply this session to your life?

Write your answers here.

1. What did God promise never to do again after the flood?

2. In what two ways do we face judgment today?

    a. _____

    b. _____

Caring Time

15-20 minutes

CARING TIME

U Remain in groups of 6-8 people, in a horseshoe configuration.

This is the time to develop and express your care for each other. Begin by asking group members to respond to this question:

> *"In what way do you need to be rescued from the flood of troubles around you?"*

Pray for strength and direction in these areas, as well as for the concerns on the Prayer/Praise Report. Include prayer for the empty chair.

If you would like to pray silently, say "Amen" when you have finished your prayer, so that the next person will know when to start.

Reference Notes

Use these notes to gain further understanding of the text as you study on your own:

GENESIS 6:11

filled with violence. The contagion introduced by Cain had become an epidemic. See Genesis 4:23 for another specific example.

GENESIS 6:14

make yourself an ark ... cover it with pitch. Another place where the Hebrew word for "ark" is used is for the basket that held baby Moses. Like Noah, Moses' mother covered her little "ark" with pitch to keep the water out (Ex. 2:3).

gofer wood. This was most likely cypress, a light and durable wood that was later used for shipbuilding by the Phoenicians.

GENESIS 6:15

450 feet long. This would have been about half as long as a modern ocean liner.

GENESIS 6:16

make a roof. God was concerned with the practical. Noah was building a boat that had to last for 40 days of rain and 150 days of floating. Because of that, air circulation had to be a concern. They could not have open areas for windows or the rain would come into the boat. This roof may have had an overhang and some open windows directly underneath it for light and air.

GENESIS 6:17

destroy all flesh under heaven. This has been understood to be a universal, worldwide flood. Some have suggested that the flood did not have to be worldwide to destroy all life because the world was so much newer and less populated. Still others say that the author was writing about the world as he knew it, the ancient Near East. Nevertheless, there was a flood, and only Noah, his family, and the animals in the ark survived.

GENESIS 6:18

establish My covenant. A covenant is an agreement, like a contract. It is a promise made between two parties. God made a covenant with Noah to save his family if Noah built the ark and entered into it by faith in God. After the flood, Noah built an altar, and God gave the rainbow as a sign that He would not destroy the earth again with a flood.

GENESIS 6:19

two of every living thing. God gave Noah two instructions about the animals to take into the ark. A pair of each animal—male and female—was needed to replenish the earth after the flood. In addition, he was to take seven pairs of the kinds of animals that could be used for eating and for sacrifice.

GENESIS 6:22

everything that God had commanded him. Noah was completely obedient. He did not cut corners, but did exactly what God said.

5

notes

6

Babel On

Genesis 11:1-9

Prepare for the Session

	READINGS	REFLECTIVE QUESTIONS
Monday	Genesis 11:1-2	What qualities or possessions have you been searching for in the migrations of your life?
Tuesday	Genesis 11:3-4	To what degree has "making a name for yourself" been an important motivation in your life? How does that motivation compare to your desire to please God?
Wednesday	Genesis 11:5-7	Is it impossible to build community with someone who speaks a different language than you do? In today's society, how can that difficulty be overcome?
Thursday	Proverbs 3:5-6	Have you been keeping yourself open to the guidance of God in making your life decisions, or have you been over-relying on self? How does God guide His followers? How has He guided you?
Friday	Acts 2:1-2	How can you keep yourself open and receptive to the power of the Holy Spirit in your life?
Saturday	Acts 2:3-6	In what ways has the Holy Spirit brought you together with other people—even across cultural barriers?
Sunday	Acts 2:7-13	How is the Spirit of God evident in your life to others around you?

BIBLE STUDY
- To better understand God's reasons for halting the Tower of Babel construction
- To understand that God really does want us to have a unified world
- To see that human abilities alone are not enough to take on the challenges of this life

LIFE CHANGE
- To commit to taking each challenge facing us to God in prayer
- To allow God to move us out of our comfort zones
- To reach out to someone outside our normal circles

Icebreaker

10-15 minutes

Now You're Talking My Language! Depending on time, choose one or two questions, or answer all three. Go around the group on question 1 and let everyone share. Then go around again on question 2 and 3.

1. What adult do you remember being able to "speak your language" when you were an adolescent?

2. How would a person "talk your language" today?

☐ Sports   ☐ Shopping or clothes
☐ Cars or mechanical things   ☐ Faith or philosophy
☐ Music (my kind!)   ☐ Books or movies
☐ Children   ☐ Politics
☐ Business   ☐ Other: _____

3. What topic of conversation has a tendency to send you packing?

☐ Sports   ☐ Shopping or clothes
☐ Cars or mechanical things   ☐ Faith or philosophy
☐ Music (not my kind!)   ☐ Books or movies
☐ Children   ☐ Politics
☐ Business   ☐ Other: _____

Bible Study

30-45 minutes

The Scripture for this week:

¹At one time the whole earth had the same language and vocabulary. ²As people migrated from the east, they found a valley in the land of Shinar and settled there. ³They said to each other, "Come, let us make oven-fired bricks." They had brick for stone and asphalt for mortar. ⁴And they said, "Come, let us build ourselves a city and a tower with its top in the sky. Let us make a name for ourselves; otherwise, we will be scattered over the face of the whole earth." ⁵Then the LORD came down to look over the city and the tower that the men were building. ⁶The LORD said, "If, as one people all having the same language, they have begun to do this, then nothing they plan to do will be impossible for them. ⁷Come, let Us go down there and confuse their language so that they will not understand one another's speech." ⁸So the LORD scattered them from there over the face of the whole earth, and they stopped building the city. ⁹Therefore its name is called Babylon, for there the LORD confused the language of the whole earth, and from there the LORD scattered them over the face of the whole earth.

6

...about today's session

A WORD
FROM THE
LEADER

**Write your
answers
here.**

1. The population of the world is now scattered over how many different countries?

2. In what two areas of the world was human population focused in the earliest time of human civilization?

    a. _____

    b. _____

3. Why did the people build the Tower of Babel?

Identifying with the Story

**Remain in groups of 6-8 people, in a horseshoe configuration.**

1. To what degree is your extended family "scattered over the face of the earth"? How does physical distance affect the emotional closeness or distance of family members?

2. When have you been involved in a project that really seemed to bring the participants together? How were people brought together?

3. Whom do you have the hardest time talking to today? Why?

   ☐ Someone from another culture
   ☐ Someone in my own family
   ☐ Someone with a different religious perspective
   ☐ People of the opposite sex
   ☐ People of my own sex
   ☐ Someone from my parents' generation
   ☐ Someone from the generation of my adult children
   ☐ Teenagers
   ☐ Other: _____

today's session

What is God teaching you from this story?

1. Besides planning the Tower of Babel, what actions have other people taken to unite humanity?

   a. _____

   b. _____

   c. _____

   d. _____

58

2. God scattered the early disciples of Jesus in a manner similar to how He scattered the people gathered to build the Tower of Babel. What did He use to do so and how is this similar to Babel?

3. What problems surface when building physically, rather than spiritually, becomes the focal point?

4. According to Paul, what foundation must be present for building a spiritual life?

Learning from the Story

6

⊍ **Remain in groups of -8 people, in a horseshoe configuration.**

1. What seems to be the main motivation the people had for building this tower? What was wrong with the motivation?

2. What concerned God about the Tower of Babel? Why did He sabotage the project in the way that He did?

3. In what way do you feel God asking you to move away from your own comfort zone?

4. How have the actions of the tower builders, although arrogant, been redeemed by God?

life change lessons

How can you
apply this
session to
your life?

Write your
answers
here.

1. Taking effective action needs to start with connecting to God for what two purposes?

   a. _____

   b. _____

2. In addition to the story of the Tower of Babel, what are some biblical stories which teach that we need to connect with God before taking action?

   a. _____

   b. _____

   c. _____

   d. _____

Caring Time
15-20 minutes

CARING
TIME

⋃ Remain
in groups of
6-8 people, in
a horseshoe
configuration.

This is the time to develop and express your care for each other. Begin by asking group members to respond to this question:

*"What direction from God do you need right now
in what you are seeking to build in your life?"*

Pray for strength and direction in these areas, as well as for the concerns on the Prayer/Praise Report. Include prayer for the empty chair.

If you would like to pray silently, say "Amen" when you have finished your prayer, so that the next person will know when to start.

Reference Notes

Use these notes to gain further understanding
of the text as you study on your own:

**GENESIS
11:1**

the whole earth. The world, as far as human population is concerned, was still relatively new. The flood had destroyed the entire human population except for Noah's family, from whom God repopulated the earth. However, it was not long before human pride resurfaced. The story of Babel is further evidence of the persistence of sinful human nature, and points to the need for an ultimate Savior.

**GENESIS
11:2**

a valley in the land of Shinar. This is the Mesopotamian valley, between the Tigris and Euphrates River.

**GENESIS
11:3**

brick. Archaeologists have discovered remnants of mud brick and tar as the choice building material of that day. The Tower of Babel was no easy architectural feat. It was most likely in the form of a ziggurat, a pyramid with giant steps or ramps leading up the side, which was a typical structure of ancient Mesopotamia (later Babylonia, now Iran or Iraq). Ziggurats as high as 300 feet have been documented.

**GENESIS
11:4**

us ... ourselves ... we. Me. Myself. I. If ever a common language of humankind were developed, it would have these three words at its core. An inordinate concern for self is the hallmark of the human race gone awry, and the architects of the tower show what happens to the human race when it gets caught up in ego. All structures made by people pale next to the power of God.

**GENESIS
11:6**

nothing they plan to do will be impossible ... Contrast this statement with what Jesus says in Matthew 17:20, "If you have faith the size of a mustard seed, you will tell this mountain, 'Move from here to there,' and it will move. Nothing will be impossible for you." It's not that God wants to limit human achievement, but rather He wants us to understand that to achieve our best we need to rely on Him and not on human strength alone.

**GENESIS
11:7**

let Us go down. The other place this plural is used for God is in the story of the creation of man in Genesis 1:26. Perhaps it was used because God was acting along with the heavenly host of angels.

confuse their language. Contrast this with the story of the birth of the Church at Pentecost, where the Holy Spirit came down and the disciples became united by God, helping them to miraculously speak each other's language (Acts 2:1-13). Pentecost was a kind of reverse Tower of Babel. The difference was that unity came by God's power and not human effort alone. This story should not then be used to say God does not want human unity.

**GENESIS
11:8**

scattered. Scattering can be a good thing. When the first disciples of Christ were scattered by persecution, it helped in the spread of the gospel (Acts 8:1). The scattering that occurred at Babel helped spread human culture beyond Mesopotamia, and forced humanity into exploring other areas with other natural resources.

6

notes

Called by a Promise

Genesis 12:1-9

Prepare for the Session

READINGS		REFLECTIVE QUESTIONS
Monday	Genesis 12:1	In what way might God be calling you to leave behind your past in order to claim the future He has for you?
Tuesday	Genesis 12:2-3	How does God want to bless other people through your life? Have you intentionally been looking for ways He could use your life to bless others?
Wednesday	Genesis 12:4	Are you willing to obey when God calls you to something difficult? Do you obey quickly, or do you need some extra prodding, some additional proof?
Thursday	Genesis 12:5-6	How well are you relating to those who are sharing in your spiritual journey?
Friday	Genesis 12:7-9	How have you shown thanks to God for His faithfulness to you?
Saturday	Hebrews 11:8	Is your faith helping you to live with the uncertainties of life? When you reach the desert, does your faith keep you strong?
Sunday	Hebrews 11:9-10	What are the promises which keep you going, which keep you confident of God's presence in your Christian walk?

7

BIBLE STUDY

- To better appreciate the necessity of obedience in fulfilling our calling
- To see how God is faithful to His promises when He calls us
- To observe the role of "deserts" on the journey to our Promised Land

LIFE CHANGE

- To evaluate our present work as a vocation
- To share our vision with those close to us
- To do something to thank God for His faithfulness

Icebreaker

10-15 minutes

GATHERING:
In groups of 6-8, gather people in a horseshoe configuration.

Moving Day. Depending on time, choose one or two questions, or answer all three. Go around the group on question 1 and let everyone share. Then go around again on question 2 and 3.

1. What was the most difficult move you remember your family having to make when you were a child or adolescent? (If you never moved, what person close to you do you remember having to move away?)

2. What is it that you most dislike about having to move?

   ☐ Leaving old friends
   ☐ All that packing and unpacking
   ☐ Leaving familiar, secure surroundings for the strange and unfamiliar
   ☐ Finding new doctors, mechanics, friends, a new church
   ☐ Having to prove myself in a new job or to new people
   ☐ The damage to my furniture
   ☐ Other: _____

3. What do you find most exciting about moving to a new place?

☐ Making new friends
☐ Experiencing new surroundings
☐ Meeting new challenges at work
☐ Getting out of old routines
☐ Leaving behind some bad memories
☐ Getting a fresh start
☐ Other: _____

Bible Study

30-45 minutes

The Scripture for this week:

¹*The LORD said to Abram: Go out from your land, your relatives, and your father's house to the land that I will show you. ²I will make you into a great nation, I will bless you, I will make your name great, and you will be a blessing. I will bless those who bless you, I will curse those who treat you with contempt, and all the peoples on earth will be blessed through you. ⁴So Abram went, as the LORD had told him, and Lot went with him. Abram was 75 years old when he left Haran. ⁵He took his wife Sarai, his nephew Lot, all the possessions they had accumulated, and the people he had acquired in Haran, and they set out for the land of Canaan. When they came to the land of Canaan, ⁶Abram passed through the land to the site of Shechem, at the oak of Moreh. At that time the Canaanites were in the land. ⁷But the LORD appeared to Abram and said, "I will give this land to your offspring." So he built an altar there to the LORD who had appeared to him. ⁸From there he moved on to the hill country east of Bethel and pitched his tent, with Bethel on the west and Ai on the east. There he built an altar to the LORD and worshiped Him. ⁹Then Abram journeyed by stages to the Negev.*

7

...about today's session

A WORD
FROM THE
LEADER

Write your
answers
here.

1. How old was Abram (Abraham) when he was called by God to go to Canaan?

2. How old was Abram when he died?

3. What was the significance of the change of Abram's name to Abraham?

Identifying with the Story

**◐ Remain
in groups of
6-8 people, in
a horseshoe
configuration.**

1. What is the closest you have come to trusting and acting on a promise like Abram does in this story?

   ☐ When I got married
   ☐ When I left a secure job for something less sure
   ☐ When I started my own business
   ☐ When I invested in a risky venture
   ☐ When I quit a steady job to go to school
   ☐ When I went into the Armed Forces
   ☐ I've never done anything like this
   ☐ Other: _____

2. Had you been Abram, what part of your life would have been the hardest to leave behind?

   ☐ The land, the environment that had nurtured me
   ☐ My family
   ☐ My "father's house"—my dependence on parental authority

66

3. As you consider your life journey to this point, what would you say has been the most significant way God has used you to bless others?

today's session

1. What did the Apostle Paul say about our calling to be a blessing to others?

2. What did Abram leave behind when he went to the Promised Land?

   a. _____

   b. _____

   c. _____

3. In what two places in the New Testament is Abraham's faith commended?

   a. _____

   b. _____

4. What two Old Testament examples are cited regarding wives who were not as supportive of their husbands as Sarai seems to have been here?

   a. _____

   b. _____

5. What desert did Abram encounter when he went to the Promised Land, and what is the meaning of its name?

7

Learning from the Story

♘ Remain in groups of 6-8 people, in a horseshoe configuration.

1. Of the promises God gave to Abram, which would you have felt to be most motivating and meaningful?

   ☐ That a "great nation" would come from me—I would have a legacy.

   ☐ Fame—I would have "a great name."

   ☐ That I would make a difference—God would bless others through me.

   ☐ That I would have protection from my enemies—God would curse those who cursed me.

   ☐ Other: _____

2. Where does Abram build altars? What do such acts say about the way Abram responded to God's promises?

3. How has God shown Himself faithful to His promises in your own life? What do you need to do to respond to that faithfulness?

life change lessons

How can you apply this session to your life?

1. What does the word "vocation" mean?

Write your answers here.

2. What similarities exist between how God used Abram's vocation and how He can use ours?

Caring Time

CARING TIME

This is the time to develop and express your care for each other. Begin by asking group members to respond to this question:

"How can God use this group right now to be a blessing to you?"

Pray for strength to bless each other in these ways. Pray also for the concerns on the Prayer/Praise Report. Include prayer for the empty chair.

If you would like to pray silently, say "Amen" when you have finished your prayer, so that the next person will know when to start.

☙ Remain in groups of -8 people, in a horseshoe configuration.

Reference Notes

BIBLE STUDY NOTES

Use these notes to gain further understanding of the text as you study on your own:

GENESIS 12:1

Go out from your land. Before there was a promising future, Abram needed to renounce his past. He first had to leave behind the familiar. Following an indirect route via the rivers, Abram left Ur to head to Haran. And from Haran he eventually settled in Canaan.

GENESIS 12:2-3

I will bless you. God did not predict Abram's future; He promised it. His promise to Abram assured him of blessing, reputation, influence, and legacy. At seventy-five years of age, who would not long to receive such a promise? However, at that time, Abram could not have imagined the extent of God's promise. Out of his descendents the entire Jewish nation and, eventually, the Savior Himself would arise.

GENESIS 12:4

Abram went. Delay was not in Abram's vocabulary. Although he was short on specific instructions, Abram packed up his belongings, got his wife and his nephew Lot, and got going. Abram's life is a model of faith in action.

GENESIS 12:5

people he had acquired. Abram's response to God's promise affected several people in the immediate picture. Of course, his family members went along for the ride. But his extended family of servants and workers who tended his wealth of flocks and herds were also affected by the news.

7

the Lord appeared. While the Lord's appearance would be an unusual event to modern readers, it was not an uncommon event for Abram. The altar became a special symbol between God and Abram. When God appeared to Abram and affirmed His promise to him, Abram often built an altar to help people remember and commemorate the experience. The stone and earthen altar would remain as a visible reminder of his journey of faith.

Bethel. About 12 miles north of Jerusalem is Bethel, a landmark in Jewish history. The site of another of Abram's altars, the city of Bethel also marked the future place of Jacob's dream with God, and housed the Ark of the Covenant for some time as well.

Negev. Abram's route took him through the Negev, literally "dry land" —referring to the southern desert wasteland. At the end of this desert trip, Abram would be eager for the resources found in the lush landscape of nearby Egypt.

Promises Fulfilled

Genesis 21:1-21

Prepare for the Session

READINGS		REFLECTIVE QUESTIONS
Monday	Genesis 21:1-2	In what ways has God been faithful to His promises to you? Have you been as faithful to Him?
Tuesday	Genesis 21:3-4	How are you personally encouraging the children in your family (immediate and/or extended) to join the family of God?
Wednesday	Genesis 21:5-7	How do you express your joy with God's wonder? How has God recently worked in your life?
Thursday	Genesis 21:8-10	When you feel threatened by the success of others, what does God call you to do?
Friday	Genesis 21:11-13	When conflicts come in your life, are you looking for solutions—solutions where all persons win?
Saturday	Genesis 21:14-16	In what ways are you "wandering in a desert" right now? Have you sought God's guidance for a way through your desert?
Sunday	Genesis 21:17-21	How has God shown you that He is with you—even during desert times? How have you thanked Him for that presence?

8

BIBLE STUDY

- To see how God was faithful in fulfilling His promises to more than just Israel
- To understand how God sometimes reveals resources to us we had never suspected were there
- To realize that part of what God promises everyone is a purpose

LIFE CHANGE

- To surrender your life direction to God in prayer
- To take the risk of exploring one new experience
- To give a little more financially to God's work than you normally do

Icebreaker
10-15 minutes

**GATHERING:
🐴 In groups
of 6-8, gather
people in a
horseshoe
configuration.**

Childhood Parties. Depending on time, choose one or two questions, or answer all three. Go around the group on question 1 and let everyone share. Then go around again on question 2 and 3.

1. If you could have designed the ideal party for yourself when you were a child, what would have been the most important part?

   ☐ Clowns
   ☐ Horses for horseback rides
   ☐ A magician
   ☐ Lots of expensive presents
   ☐ All friends and no "have to" invitees!
   ☐ Cool games only—nothing lame
   ☐ Going to a special place like a ball game or concert
   ☐ Going to a theme park with lots of roller coasters
   ☐ Other: _____

2. What was the quickest way for someone to "spoil the party"?

☐ A parent getting angry
☐ Friends fighting for attention
☐ A parent babying me
☐ Presents getting broken
☐ Little brothers or sisters stealing the show
☐ A jealous sibling messing things up
☐ Other: _____

3. When you have something to celebrate *today*, what is most likely to "spoil the party"?

☐ Someone else's jealousy
☐ My own negativism
☐ Lack of time due to other responsibilities
☐ Lack of the kind of funds it takes to *really* celebrate
☐ Something else going wrong
☐ Other: _____

Bible Study

30-45 minutes

The Scripture for this week:

LEARNING FROM THE BIBLE

GENESIS 21:1-21

¹*The* LORD *came to Sarah as He had said, and the* LORD *did for Sarah what He had promised.* ²*Sarah became pregnant and bore a son to Abraham in his old age, at the appointed time God had told him.* ³*Abraham named his son who was born to him—the one Sarah bore to him—Isaac.* ⁴*When his son Isaac was eight days old, Abraham circumcised him, as God had commanded him.* ⁵*Abraham was 100 years old when his son Isaac was born to him.* ⁶*Sarah said, "God has made me laugh, and everyone who hears will laugh with me."* ⁷*She also said, "Who would have told Abraham that Sarah would nurse children? Yet I have borne him a son in his old age."* ⁸*The child grew and was weaned, and Abraham held a great feast on the day Isaac was weaned.* ⁹*But Sarah saw the son mocking—the one Hagar the Egyptian had borne to Abraham.* ¹⁰*So she said to Abraham, "Drive out this slave with her son, for the son of*

this slave will not be a co-heir with my son Isaac!" [11]*Now this was a very difficult thing for Abraham because of his son.* [12]*But God said to Abraham, "Do not be concerned about the boy and your slave. Whatever Sarah says to you, listen to her, because your offspring will be traced through Isaac.* [13]*But I will also make a nation of the slave's son because he is your offspring."* [14]*Early in the morning Abraham got up, took bread and a waterskin, put them on Hagar's shoulders, and sent her and the boy away. She left and wandered in the Wilderness of Beer-sheba.* [15]*When the water in the skin was gone, she left the boy under one of the bushes.* [16]*Then she went and sat down nearby, about a bowshot away, for she said, "I can't bear to watch the boy die!" So as she sat nearby, she wept loudly.* [17]*God heard the voice of the boy, and the angel of God called to Hagar from heaven and said to her, "What's wrong, Hagar? Don't be afraid, for God has heard the voice of the boy from the place where he is.* [18]*Get up, help the boy up, and sustain him, for I will make him a great nation."* [19]*Then God opened her eyes, and she saw a well of water. So she went and filled the waterskin and gave the boy a drink.* [20]*God was with the boy, and he grew; he settled in the wilderness and became an archer.* [21]*He settled in the Wilderness of Paran, and his mother got a wife for him from the land of Egypt.*

...about today's session

A WORD
FROM THE
LEADER

Write your
answers
here.

1. What people trace their ancestry to Abraham through Ishmael?

2. Why is it especially significant that this story was preserved in Scripture?

3. What two Scripture passages help us see that God chose Israel not just for themselves, but to be a blessing to other countries?

   a. _____

   b. _____

Identifying with the Story

⛊ Remain in groups of -8 people, in a horseshoe configuration.

1. When Sarah gave birth to Isaac in her old age, she said, "God has made me laugh." What has happened to you recently that has made you shake your head in amazement or laugh as a result of God's hard-to-believe ways of working in your life?

2. What aspect of your own life story is most like Hagar's?

   ☐ I've felt victimized by other people's jealousy (v. 10).
   ☐ I've been "sent packing" with inadequate child support (bread and a water skin!) (v. 14).
   ☐ I've done my share of wandering in a wilderness (v. 14).
   ☐ I've felt the fear that I wasn't able to protect my loved ones (vv. 15-16).
   ☐ God has provided resources for me that I had never suspected were there (v. 19).
   ☐ Other: _____

3. When did God reveal resources you needed that you previously had overlooked? How did this experience change your outlook?

8

today's session

What is God teaching you from this story?

1. What are three areas where God is faithful in fulfilling promises?

   a. _____

   b. _____

   c. _____

2. Compare Sarah's laughter before Isaac's birth to after it. How did the tone of her laughter change?

3. What does the name "Ishmael" mean?

4. Give two biblical passages that tell us God is not one to show favoritism?

    a. _____

    b. _____

5. What rationale seems to be behind the distribution of spiritual gifts?

Learning from the Story

1. Why do you think God urged Abraham to do what Sarah asked of him in regard to Ishmael?

    ☐ He knew He could protect Ishmael.
    ☐ He knew that keeping them all together wouldn't work, considering all the jealousy
    ☐ He wanted Sarah and Abraham to be able to get along.
    ☐ Hagar and Ishmael needed to have their own separate life.
    ☐ Isaac needed to be established as the primary heir.
    ☐ Other: _____

2. Why do you think Hagar hadn't seen the well of water before she did?

☐ God was hiding it to test her faith.
☐ In her grief she was "blind" to good fortune.
☐ God just then miraculously created it.
☐ God wanted to reveal it as an expression of His love.
☐ Other: _____

3. In what way(s) do you feel like you have exhausted all your resources, and need God to guide you to a "well"?

life change lessons

How can you apply this session to your life?

1. How do we show that we truly believe God's promises?

Write your answers here.

2. How did the people in this week's lesson show that they believed what God had promised?

    a. _____

    b. _____

8

Caring Time

15-20 minutes

**CARING
TIME**

⚘ **Remain
in groups of
6-8 people, in
a horseshoe
configuration.**

This is the time to develop and express your care for each other. Begin by asking group members to respond to this question:

*"For what struggle are you needing God
to show you new resources right now?"*

Pray for God's strength in these struggles, as well as praying for the concerns on the Prayer/Praise Report. Include prayer for the empty chair.

If you would like to pray silently, say "Amen" when you have finished your prayer, so that the next person will know when to start.

**BIBLE
STUDY
NOTES**

Reference Notes

Use these notes to gain further understanding
of the text as you study on your own:

**GENESIS
21:1**

did ... what He had promised. Finally, the impossible promise came true (Gen. 15:4; 17:15-19).

**GENESIS
21:3**

Isaac. The name means, "He laughs." Abraham once laughed, scoffing at the idea of fathering a son at his age (Gen. 17:17). Sarah had laughed, too (Gen. 18:12). This time the laughter was happier.

**GENESIS
21:5**

Isaac was born. God promised Abraham, now 100 years old, that he would be the father of a son by Sarah (Gen. 17:16).

**GENESIS
21:9**

the one Hagar the Egyptian had borne. This refers to Ishmael, born to Abraham by Hagar. That such an act would happen was part of accepted practice when a wife was barren, and was suggested by Sarah herself (see Gen. 16:1-16).

**GENESIS
21:10**

this slave with her son. Sarah didn't want her son to share his inheritance. Somehow it didn't matter to her any more that she had suggested the whole arrangement. In fact, previously she had seen Ishmael as part of her family. When she made the proposal she had said, "Perhaps I can have children by her" (Gen. 16:2). Now, however, she saw Ishmael as Hagar's son, not hers and not Abraham's.

GENESIS 21:11 *a very difficult thing for Abraham.* Abraham was concerned that Ishmael would have a very difficult life being the estranged son of a servant woman.

GENESIS 21:12 *Whatever Sarah says ... listen to her.* God calms Abraham's fears somewhat by promising that both Isaac and Ishmael would father great nations. Nevertheless, God's plan for Abraham's descendents would unfold through Isaac's line.

GENESIS 21:14 *Early in the morning.* Despite certain anxiety, Abraham obeyed God's command immediately, even though it meant being away from Ishmael.
bread and a waterskin. If Abraham can be faulted in this situation, it would be in this inadequate provision. Surely a man of some wealth who was concerned about his son and his son's mother could have done better.

GENESIS 21:17 *God heard ... God has heard.* The name Ishmael means, "God hears."

GENESIS 21:19 *God opened her eyes.* Hagar's grief was so deep that God had to open her eyes so she could see the much-needed water. The Old Testament often uses a spring or water well to symbolize both spiritual and physical salvation.

GENESIS 21:21 *his mother got a wife for him from the land of Egypt.* Hagar was herself from Egypt, so she made sure her son married within her heritage.

8

notes

The Presence of God

Genesis 28:10-22

Prepare for the Session

	READINGS	REFLECTIVE QUESTIONS
Monday	Genesis 28:10-11	How adaptable are you at work or at home when you have to face less-than-ideal circumstances? How does God help you adapt?
Tuesday	Genesis 28:12-13	How does God speak to people today? Has God ever spoken to you through a dream? If so, how did you respond?
Wednesday	Genesis 28:14-15	How has God blessed your family? How has God used your family to bless others?
Thursday	Genesis 28:16-17	Where have you encountered God in the past week? How would you describe that encounter?
Friday	Genesis 28:18-19	At what places has God really changed your life?
Saturday	Genesis 28:20-22	Are you as faithful to your promises to God as God is in His promises to you? What vows have you made to God as an act of worship? How well have you done in keeping those vows?
Sunday	Acts 17:26-28	Do you feel that God is near to you right now? If not, what can you do to more fully gain a sense of His nearness or closeness?

9

BIBLE STUDY
- To better appreciate how God's presence can be experienced in nature
- To understand that God is present in all places and at all times
- To explore what our response should be to God's faithfulness in being present with us

LIFE CHANGE
- To spend quiet time in a natural setting
- To spend time each day looking for evidences of God's presence
- To identify and establish spiritual markers in life.

Icebreaker

10-15 minutes

GATHERING:
In groups
of 6-8, gather
people in a
horseshoe
configuration.

Camping Out. Depending on time, choose one or two questions, or answer all three. Go around the group on question 1 and let everyone share. Then go around again on question 2 and 3.

1. Which of the following kinds of "camping out" experiences did you have as a child or adolescent?

   ☐ Being in Boy Scouts, Girl Scouts, or a similar group
   ☐ Tent camping with friends or family
   ☐ Backpacking in wilderness areas
   ☐ Setting up a tent in our back yard
   ☐ Camping in a tent trailer or RV
   ☐ Going to a church camp
   ☐ "Camping out" while waiting for concert tickets
   ☐ Waiting for the mall to open is the closest I ever came
   ☐ Other: _____

2. What would you say is your present attitude toward "roughing it" outdoors?

   ☐ The more primitive the wilderness, the better.
   ☐ Roadside camps only, please.
   ☐ Running water and real rest rooms ... "roughing it" means "sleeping outside"

- [ ] Anywhere I can take my RV
- [ ] A rustic cabin with a fireplace
- [ ] A motel—but without premium movie channels!
- [ ] Other: _____

3. When you are in a situation where you are "roughing it," what do you miss the most?

- [ ] My own bed
- [ ] My favorite television shows
- [ ] A nice warm shower
- [ ] Protection from the elements
- [ ] A clean environment
- [ ] My mind—because it drives me crazy!
- [ ] Other: _____ _____

Bible Study

30-45 minutes

The Scriptures for this week:

LEARNING FROM THE BIBLE

GENESIS 28:10-22

[10]*Jacob left Beer-sheba and went toward Haran.* [11]*He reached a certain place and spent the night there because the sun had set. He took one of the stones from the place, put it there at his head, and lay down in that place.* [12]*And he dreamed: A stairway was set on the ground with its top reaching heaven, and God's angels were going up and down on it.* [13]*The LORD was standing there beside him, saying, "I am the LORD, the God of your father Abraham and the God of Isaac. I will give you and your offspring the land that you are now sleeping on.* [14]*Your offspring will be like the dust of the earth, and you will spread out toward the west, the east, the north, and the south. All the peoples on earth will be blessed through you and your offspring.* [15]*Look, I am with you and will watch over you wherever you go. I will bring you back to this land, for I will not leave you until I have done what I have promised you."* [16]*When Jacob awoke from his sleep, he said, "Surely the LORD is in this place, and I did not know it."* [17]*He was afraid and said, "What an awesome place*

9

this is! This is none other than the house of God. This is the gate of heaven." ¹⁸Early in the morning Jacob took the stone that was near his head and set it up as a marker. He poured oil on top of it ¹⁹and named the place Bethel, though previously the city was named Luz. ²⁰Then Jacob made a vow: "If God will be with me and watch over me on this journey, if He provides me with food to eat and clothing to wear, ²¹and if I return safely to my father's house, then the LORD will be my God. ²²This stone that I have set up as a marker will be God's house, and I will give to You a tenth of all that You give me."

...about today's session

1. Where do we get the idea that heaven is entered through pearly gates?

2. How is the stairway in the story of Jacob at Bethel different from the stairway in the other story?

3. How do we find the gates of heaven for ourselves?

Identifying with the Story

1. What is the most revelational dream you remember having? Did you sense a message of any kind? If so, explain?

2. At what physical locations do you recall sensing the presence and power of God most profoundly? What characteristics of the place gave you that feeling?

3. What promises have you made to God as the result of some strange or frightening experience?

today's session

1. In what three ways did the ancient religions answer the question, Where is God?

   a. _____

   b. _____

   c. _____

2. In what other scriptural stories did people encounter God in natural settings? Can you think of others?

   a. _____

   b. _____

   c. _____

   d. _____

   e. _____

3. What surprised Jacob about the actual location of his experience at Bethel?

9

4. What two promises did God make to Jacob in his dream?

   a. _____

   b. _____

5. God promised to be with Jacob wherever he went (v. 15). What events in Jacob's journey show God's faithfulness to keep that promise?

   a. _____

   b. _____

   c. _____

   d. _____

   e. _____

Learning from the Story

⟲ **Remain
in groups of
6-8 people, in
a horseshoe
configuration.**

1. What was Jacob "afraid" of after this vision (v. 17)?

   ☐ That he would disappoint God
   ☐ That maybe he was going crazy
   ☐ All the responsibility
   ☐ The majesty and power of God
   ☐ The supernatural aspects of the dream
   ☐ Other: _____

2. What do you think of the conditions Jacob places on his vow to God in verses 20-22?

   ☐ He was expecting God to baby him too much.
   ☐ He was showing a lack of faith by placing any conditions on his vow at all.
   ☐ He was only expecting what God had already promised.
   ☐ Other: _____

3. If God gave you the promises He gave to Jacob, and you truly believed those promises, how would it affect how you lived your life?

life change lessons

How can you apply this session to your life?

Write your answers here.

1. In what incidents does Jacob show himself to be less than noble in character?

    a. _____

    b. _____

2. In what two actions did Jacob later show himself faithful to his promise to God?

    a. _____

    b. _____

Caring Time

15-20 minutes 9

CARING TIME

⋃ **Remain in groups of 5-8 people, in a horseshoe configuration.**

This is the time to develop and express your care for each other. Begin by asking group members to respond to this question:

"How have you experienced God's presence through what has happened in this group?"

Thank God for these experiences; and then pray for the concerns on the Prayer/Praise Report. Include prayer for the empty chair.

If you would like to pray silently, say "Amen" when you have finished your prayer, so that the next person will know when to start.

Reference Notes

Use these notes to gain further understanding
of the text as you study on your own:

**GENESIS
28:11**

He took one of the stones. As strange as it sounds, this made a more comfortable bed for Jacob. People traveled only with a cloak and some food, using the hard ground for a bed.

**GENESIS
28:12**

stairway. We may sing about "Jacob's ladder," but he probably saw a stairway.

God's angels ... on it. In this dream, God demonstrated that He wanted a relationship with Jacob, that He wanted to be not only the God of his grandfather Abraham and his father Isaac, but of Jacob as well.

**GENESIS
28:13**

The Lord was standing there. Despite the language here, we don't need to think of God standing up on two legs like a human being. This just indicates that He was present in some kind of visible way at the stairway. This Lord was inviting Jacob into a relationship with Him.

**GENESIS
28:14**

All the peoples on earth. God had said these words to Jacob's grandfather, Abraham (Gen. 12:3). He had then said them to his father, Isaac (Gen. 26:4), and now He was repeating them to Jacob. Note that the covenant would not just be a blessing to Israel, but to "all the peoples."

**GENESIS
28:15**

I am with you. God had made this promise to Isaac as well (Gen. 26:3).

I will not leave you. It did not matter where Jacob went, the one true God would be with him. Jacob was running away from all that he knew, but he could not run from what God had planned for him.

**GENESIS
28:17**

house of God. Wherever God is found is His home. Later Israel would build a Temple and call it God's house, and sometimes today we call our church buildings "God's house." But in this session's Scripture passage, we find that God's presence can be found in the most remote and empty desert, and that place is God's house.

**GENESIS
28:18**

marker. At this location, Jacob's grandfather, Abraham, had built an altar and called on the name of the Lord (Gen. 12:7). Jacob took the stone on which he had slept and consecrated it with oil to remember what had occurred at this spot.

**GENESIS
28:20**

vow. Jacob's promise of faithfulness to God was conditional. He desired to be cared for on his lonely journey and to return safely. He knew nothing more about this God who had revealed Himself, but he was open to following Him. God did bring Jacob safely back to Bethel, where Jacob built an altar to Him (Gen. 35:1-15).

This stone. The stone would be a reminder of Jacob's meeting with God at Bethel, and Jacob never forgot the power of this meeting (Gen. 35:3,6).

a tenth of all that You give me. This was a tangible way for Jacob to acknowledge the Lord as his God. The tenth, or tithe, was seen in Abraham's gift to Melchizedek the priest (Gen. 14:20), and later was required by the Mosaic Law (Deut. 14:22).

9

notes

Wrestling with God

Genesis 32:22-32

Prepare for the Session

	READINGS	REFLECTIVE QUESTIONS
Monday	Genesis 32:22-23	What would you do if right now God called you to pull up roots and move somewhere else?
Tuesday	Genesis 32:24	With which relationships do you seem to be "wrestling" right now? In what ways does it feel you are struggling in the dark?
Wednesday	Genesis 32:25	How have your conflicts with God and others wounded you? What do you need to do to find healing?
Thursday	Genesis 32:26-27	What are you having a hard time letting go of right now?
Friday	Genesis 32:27-28	Do you feel like you are prevailing in your life right now—or letting circumstances control you? What blessing do you need from God to keep (or get) on top of those tough situations in your life?
Saturday	Genesis 32:29-30	How have you seen God in the events of your life this past week?
Sunday	Genesis 32:31-32	In what ways have you felt the sun shine in your life in the past few months? What have you done to show your gratitude to God?

10

OUR GOALS FOR THIS SESSION ARE:

BIBLE STUDY

· To better understand what it means to wrestle with God in a spiritual sense
· To appreciate the blessing we can find when we wrestle with the issues that confuse us in relation to God
· To think through and understand the difference between those times when we must wrestle with problems alone, and when we need to ask for help

LIFE CHANGE

· To set aside some "wrestling" time
· To talk to one other person who is struggling in a similar way
· To ask your pastor to deliver a sermon series in the area where you are struggling

Icebreaker

10-15 minutes

GATHERING: In groups of 6-8, gather people in a horseshoe configuration.

Mano a Mano. Depending on time, choose one or two questions, or answer all three. Go around the group on question 1 and let everyone share. Then go around again on question 2 and 3.

1. When you were an adolescent, how likely were you to go "mano a mano" (face-to-face confrontation) with someone?

☐ In my school/neighborhood, it was almost an everyday event.
☐ Well, I had a reputation to protect.
☐ With girls, it was more like hand to hair combat.
☐ Mostly it was with a bully who provoked me.
☐ OK, maybe *I* was the bully.
☐ My fighting was more sophisticated—I was master of the cutting remark!
☐ I only fought when provoked.
☐ I was a lover, not a fighter.
☐ Other: _____

2. When you went *mano a mano* with someone at that age, what was it likely to be over?

    ☐ The opposite sex
    ☐ People spreading gossip about me
    ☐ Defending a family member
    ☐ The old lunch money problem
    ☐ Just proving who could take whom
    ☐ Other: _____

3. Figuratively or literally, who are you most likely to go *mano a mano* with today?

    ☐ My spouse or significant other
    ☐ A rival at work
    ☐ An extended family member or in-law
    ☐ A teenage son or daughter
    ☐ Government officials
    ☐ An irritating neighbor
    ☐ Other: _____

Bible Study

30-45 minutes

The Scripture for this week:

LEARNING FROM THE BIBLE

GENESIS 32:22-32

[10]

²²During the night Jacob got up and took his two wives, his two female slaves, and his 11 sons, and crossed the ford of Jabbok. ²³He took them and brought them across the stream, along with all his possessions. ²⁴Jacob was left alone, and a man wrestled with him until daybreak. ²⁵When the man saw that He could not defeat him, He struck Jacob's hip as they wrestled and dislocated his hip socket. ²⁶Then He said to Jacob, "Let Me go, for it is daybreak." But Jacob said, "I will not let You go unless You bless me." ²⁷"What is your name?" the man asked. "Jacob!" he replied. ²⁸"Your name will no longer be Jacob," He said. "It will be Israel because you have struggled with God and with men and have prevailed." ²⁹Then Jacob asked Him, "Please tell me Your name." But He answered, "Why do

you ask My name?" And He blessed him there. ³⁰Jacob then named the place Peniel, "For," he said, "I have seen God face to face, and I have been delivered." ³¹The sun shone on him as he passed by Penuel—limping on his hip. ³²That is why, to this day, the Israelites don't eat the thigh muscle that is at the hip socket: because He struck Jacob's hip socket at the thigh muscle.

...about today's session

1. What are some explanations for the wrestling scene? What do you think?

2. What other four biblical stories include angels being mistaken for men?

   a. _____

   b. _____

   c. _____

   d. _____

3. The first angels referenced in Scripture are commissioned to do what?

4. Give two possible reasons why Jacob was able to last so long in wrestling with this angel.

   a. _____

   b. _____

Identifying with the Story

1. With what issues are you currently "wrestling"?

   ☐ Does God exist?
   ☐ Is Christianity the best way to find God?
   ☐ Why do evil things happen?
   ☐ Has God uniquely suited me for a purpose?
   ☐ How can I know God better?
   ☐ Does God really pursue a relationship with me?
   ☐ Is God safe?
   ☐ Other: _____

2. In what ways have you been wounded during prior "wrestling" matches? How did you respond?

3. How has God recently blessed you? If you could rename yourself based on this blessing, what might your name be?

today's session

What is God
teaching you
from this
story?

1. What biblical character questioned whether God played fair in their spiritual "wrestling match"?

10

2. Why must we sometimes wrestle with God alone?

3. What was the significance of Jacob's name change from "Jacob" to "Israel"?

4. Give two ways people sometimes seek to avoid a struggle with God.

   a. _____

   b. _____

5. What did Jacob call the place where he wrestled with the angel? What is the significance of that name?

Learning from the Story

↻ **Remain in groups of 6-8 people, in a horseshoe configuration.**

1. When do you think Jacob first realized he was wrestling with was an angel of God?

   ☐ Right from the get-go
   ☐ Once the angel struck his hip
   ☐ When the angel blessed him
   ☐ When the angel wouldn't give his name
   ☐ When the angel proved to be so strong
   ☐ Other: _____

2. The angel asked why Jacob wanted to know His name. What do you think the answer was?

   ☐ Jacob wanted the name in order to brag to his friends.
   ☐ It seemed like the thing to do since the angel had asked his name.
   ☐ He wanted to confirm that he really was wrestling with an angel.
   ☐ It was just his natural curiosity.
   ☐ Other: _____

3. Where are you currently in your "wrestling" with God?

☐ Standing in my corner, not yet introduced
☐ In the early stages
☐ In the toughest part of fray
☐ Worn out from the struggle, approaching morning
☐ Wounded by God
☐ Receiving my blessing
☐ I yielded in the match long ago
☐ Other: _____

life change lessons

How can you apply this session to your life?

Write your answers here.

1. What are three important strategies in our wrestling match with God?

   a. _____

   b. _____

   c. _____

2. What does it mean to "respect the opponent" in our wrestling with God?

Caring Time
15-20 minutes

CARING TIME

♘ **Remain in groups of -8 people, in a horseshoe configuration.**

This is the time to develop and express your care for each other. Begin by asking group members to respond to this question:

"How has this group blessed you during the time we have been 'wrestling' together?"

Thank God for these blessings, as well as praying for the concerns on the Prayer/Praise Report. Include prayer for the empty chair.

If you would like to pray silently, say "Amen" when you have finished your prayer, so that the next person will know when to start.

10

Reference Notes

Use these notes to gain further understanding
of the text as you study on your own:

**GENESIS
32:24**

left alone. When we are concerned about our life and the future, there is
no more vulnerable place to be than alone with our God.

wrestled. Jacob was known as a "heel grabber" (Gen. 25:24-26). He
attempted to pin Esau to the mat early in his life. He wrestled Laban to
gain an advantage, and now he attempted to twist God's arm. He would
learn who held ultimate control over his life.

**GENESIS
32:25**

dislocated his hip socket. Jacob could wrestle with God. Yet God, with
one touch, revealed that He had the ultimate power.

**GENESIS
32:26**

not...unless You bless me. Jacob was not penalized for holding. Rather,
his unwavering persistence is a positive example. Hanging on to God
for dear life is a key to blessing. Jacob realized that if he was going to be
blessed, God would have to do it.

**GENESIS
32:28**

Israel. The name "Jacob" meant, "he deceives" (Gen. 27:36); but this new
name "Israel" meant, "he struggled with God." The old name fit his old
character, as when he deceived his father and brother. But his new name
fit his new character. The nation that was descended from him also would
take that name appropriately, since the nation of Israel struggled with God
during their entire history.

**GENESIS
32:29**

Why do you ask My name? Speaking of names, Jacob wondered about
the name of Him who had given him a new name. Moses also had oppor-
tunity to ask God His name (Ex. 3:13-14). But His response reminds us
that God cannot be reduced to a name. He is the one and only God, and
does not need a name to differentiate Himself from others.

**GENESIS
32:30**

Peniel. The name means "face of God."
I have been delivered. Moses was told that no human being could see
God's face and live (Ex. 33:20); and the prophet Isaiah feared for his life
because of this, but was also "delivered" (Isa. 6:5-7).

notes

10

notes

11

Forgiving a Brother

Genesis 33:1-11

Prepare for the Session

	READINGS	REFLECTIVE QUESTIONS
Monday	Genesis 33:1-3	What signs of danger do you see coming your way? Do you feel prepared for them?
Tuesday	Genesis 33:4	Those persons who have hurt you deeply—are you able to forgive them with a passion and enthusiasm that is real?
Wednesday	Genesis 33:5-7	How do you credit God for all the blessings you enjoy? What is your favorite way of showing gratitude?
Thursday	Genesis 33:8-9	How do you let your actions reflect simple gratitude for what God has given to you?
Friday	Genesis 33:10	Whose forgiveness has particularly touched you in your life? What did that person have to overcome to forgive in this way?
Saturday	Genesis 33:11	Have you been willing to share what God has graciously provided for you? Can you give without expecting anything in return?
Sunday	Matthew 6:14-15	If God forgave you according to the forgiveness you have shown others, where would that leave you?

11

OUR GOALS FOR THIS SESSION ARE:

BIBLE STUDY
- To explore how forgiving others and being forgiven helps us experience God
- To think through what it means to forgive from the heart enthusiastically
- To better understand the role forgiveness plays within a family

LIFE CHANGE
- To pray that God will lead you to those you need to forgive
- To contact a family member you have had a conflict with in the past
- To write a letter to a deceased person you need to forgive

Icebreaker

10-15 minutes

GATHERING: In groups of 6-8, gather people in a horseshoe configuration.

Family Reunions. Depending on time, choose one or two questions, or answer all three. Go around the group on question 1 and let everyone share. Then go around again on question 2 and 3.

1. When you think about your last family reunion, what comes to mind?

   ☐ The Hatfields and the McCoys—It's a family feud
   ☐ Reunited—It was so good to see everybody again
   ☐ Pass the barbeque—My family loves to eat
   ☐ As time goes by—I just can't believe how much everyone has changed
   ☐ Houston, we have a problem—I never realized how different my family was from others
   ☐ Endless summer—I remember the wonderful days of my childhood

2. Describe the best family reunion you have ever attended? What made the experience good?

3. When you reunite with your extended family, what family member do you *least* look forward to seeing? What makes this relationship a tense one for you?

Bible Study

The Scripture for this week:

¹*Now Jacob looked up and saw Esau coming toward him with 400 men. So he divided the children among Leah, Rachel, and the two female slaves. ²He put the female slaves first, Leah and her sons next, and Rachel and Joseph last. ³He himself went on ahead and bowed to the ground seven times until he approached his brother. ⁴But Esau ran to meet him, hugged him, threw his arms around him, and kissed him. Then they wept. ⁵When Esau looked up and saw the women and children, he asked, "Who are these with you?" He answered, "The children God has graciously given your servant." ⁶Then the female slaves and their children approached him and bowed down. ⁷Leah and her children also approached and bowed down, and then Joseph and Rachel approached and bowed down. ⁸So Esau said, "What do you mean by this whole procession I met?" "To find favor with you, my lord," he answered. ⁹"I have enough, my brother," Esau replied. "Keep what you have." ¹⁰But Jacob said, "No, please! If I have found favor with you, take this gift from my hand. For indeed, I have seen your face, and it is like seeing God's face, since you have accepted me. ¹¹Please take my present that was brought to you, because God has been gracious to me and I have everything I need." So Jacob urged him until he accepted.*

11

...about today's session

A WORD
FROM THE
LEADER

Write your
answers
here.

1. What does Scripture state as one of the best ways for us to reflect our godly image?

2. What previous experience was Jacob probably thinking about when he told Esau that seeing his face was like seeing the face of God?

3. What New Testament Scriptures underscore the connection between forgiving our brothers and sisters and experiencing God?

   a. _____

   b. _____

   c. _____

   d. _____

Identifying with the Story

1. Although it's understandable, Jacob approached Esau with hesitancy. Think about a confrontation that you approached with similar hesistancy or even dread. How did it turn out?

2. How do you generally react when someone sends you a gift to diminish his guilt or to smooth the way to reconciliation?

   ☐ "Don't think you can buy me!"

   ☐ Depends—are we talking cars or fruitcake?

   ☐ It can earn them an "audience," but it doesn't solve the problem.

   ☐ I'm easy—ice cream or candy heals all wounds.

☐ Well, at least it shows an effort.

☐ Other: _____

3. When have you been touched to an extent such as Jacob's at Esau's forgiveness?

today's session

1. What early heresy stated that the God of the Old Testament was really a different God than the God of the New Testament?

2. What are some parallels between the story of Jacob and Esau and the Parable of the Prodigal Son?

   a. _____

   b. _____

   c. _____

   d. _____

   e. _____

3. To what "far country" did Jacob flee and why?

4. How is Esau different from the elder son in the Parable of the Prodigal Son?

5. What does Jesus say about the spirit with which we need to forgive our brothers and sisters?

11

105

Learning from the Story

♘Remain in groups of 6-8 people, in a horseshoe configuration.

1. Given that Esau had forgiven Jacob, why do you think he was coming Jacob's way with 400 men?

   ☐ To show what he *could* have done if he had wanted to
   ☐ In case Jacob meant harm to *him*
   ☐ Maybe he hadn't fully made up his mind to forgive.
   ☐ Maybe these men were just for protection from others along the way.
   ☐ Other: _____

2. To whom does Jacob give the credit for the good things that had happened in his life? Why was it important for him to do this in the situation?

3. What would you have to put behind you in order to forgive as Esau forgave? What help would you need to do this?

life change lessons

How can you apply this session to your life?

1. What had Jacob and Esau's parents done to set up their lifelong conflict?

Write your answers here.

2. What threefold progression of action can we see in the story of Jacob and Esau?

   a. _____

   b. _____

   c. _____